**To order additional copies of this study,
visit www.StoneSoupforFive.com or Amazon.com.**

Editor: Kristen He
Illustrations: Kari Denker

Printed in the United States of America

First Printing, 2016

Why study the prophecies of Scripture over Christmas? Why study them at all?

There are plenty of deep scholarly reasons to study the prophecies, and to study them deeper than we will in this guide, but today in our hectic lives, we need to know and remember that Jesus is EXACTLY who He said He is. He is the unchangeable Messiah of the Old Testament, the Savior of the New Testament, and Creator God who seeks those He loves and provides a way back to Him.

In today's skeptical world where questioning everything is the norm (and even applauded) we need lots of reminders. Just as the men and women in the Old Testament kept hearing again and again the promises from God through the prophets, we need to hear those today as well.

Nothing has spun out of control, nothing (not your sin, not mine, not theirs) has ruined God's sovereign plan for His creation and His people. We need to be reminded that God cannot be moved, and does not change (Psalm 15). We need to remember that He is the suffering Servant, willing to die for our sins (Isaiah 53), but He is also the everlasting, reigning King over all creation, forever and ever; despite what the newspaper or doctor's report says. We need a new infusion of hope and assurance that God does exactly what He promises.

This Christmas season, I pray your hope will be renewed afresh at the awesomeness of our God and Savior. And if you enjoy your time in this short introduction into the prophecies of the Messiah, I hope you'll continue to dig deep into all the prophecies and Bible history that will back up the truthfulness and faithfulness of our Lord and Savior, the Wonderful Counselor, the Mighty God, Eternal Father, Prince of Peace.

Creating Your Own Advent Journal

You can work through this study in a number of ways:
You can read through the daily pages and color the coloring pages in this journal, looking up and reading each reference for the prophecies and fulfillments.

Or you can also make your own advent journal using the doodle prompts on each page. This will give you more room to journal your thoughts and make your own, personal journal to treasure.

You can also do this with your children, printing off coloring pages for them to color along with you or using the advent grid for them to search for the picture of the day and color it in.

No matter which method you choose, be sure you enjoy the time, reflect on the season, and draw close to the Messiah, our Savior, Christ the Lord.

Below are the list of prophecies we will be studying through this Christmas season. If you have time, read each of the prophecies about the Messiah and write a brief description of those prophecies in your own words. What qualities do these verses say the Messiah will have? What will He do? What will happen to Him?

Write out who you think Messiah will be according to these verses. Put yourself in the shoes of the Jewish people who studied these Scriptures before Jesus was born. Who were they looking for? How did so many miss Him?

the prophecies

Genesis 3:15

*

Genesis 12:3
Genesis 17:7-8
Genesis 26:2-4
Numbers 24:17-19

*

Isaiah 9:6

*

Isaiah 7:13-14

*

Isaiah 9:7
Psalm 132:11
Jeremiah 23:5-6

*

Micah 5:2-5

*

Psalm 72:5-11

*

Isaiah 40:3-5
Malachi 3:1

Deuteronomy 18:15
Deuteronomy 18:18-19

*

Psalms 78:2
Isaiah 6:9-10

*

Zechariah 9:9-10
Psalms 118:25-26

*

Isaiah 28:16
Zechariah 10:4

*

Psalms 2:1-2
Psalms 69:9
Psalms 118:22-23
Isaiah 53

*

Psalms 41:9
Zechariah 11:12

*

Zechariah 11:12-13

*

Isaiah 53:8

Isaiah 53:7-8

*

Micah 5:1
Isaiah 50:6-7

*

Psalms 22:1, 14-16

*

Psalms 22:1, 18, 53

*

Numbers 9:12
Psalms 22:17

*

Isaiah 53:5-6, 8, 10-12

*

Isaiah 53:9

*

Psalms 16:10
Psalms 30:3
Psalms 110:1

day one: the first promise...

God has always had a plan. He is a God who seeks those He created and longs to have a relationship with us.
No sin has ever changed that.
When sin entered the picture, God already had a plan to remove it from us as far as the east is from the west!

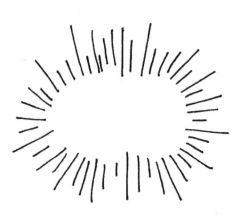

CHRISTMAS CHALLENGE

Throughout this study we'll have some fun and simple challenges. Join in on any you want and have fun! It's meant to add some affordable and simple fun to your Advent celebration!

day one ...the first promise

The first promise of a Savior, or Messiah, was given in Genesis 3:15. But before we jump in to the prophecy, let's look at the context. God had just created the brand new world. Everything in it was perfect and good. No death, no disease, no weeds, it was fresh, new and exciting. Adam was created in God's image and given enjoyable work to do. He had a perfect wife and all their needs provided for. They walked with God, talked with God, and lived in paradise.

But a fruit was considered, coveted, and taken against the will of God. Immediately their relationship with God was tainted and death was the consequence. But God, being just and merciful, covered them, provided for them, and immediately gave the hope-filled promise of a Savior to come.

Prophecy: Genesis 3:15

"What was the death that was threatened to Adam? 'In the day that thou eatest thereof thou shalt surely die.' Is death annihilation? Was Adam annihilated that day? Assuredly not: he lived many a year afterwards. But in the day in which he ate of the forbidden fruit he died, by being separated from God. The separation of the soul from God is spiritual death; just as the separation of the soul from the body is natural death." -C. H. Spurgeon

Read Genesis 3:15 (or the entire chapter). Here is the hope-filled promise of a Savior. A Messiah. A snake-crusher who will forever put an end to the enmity with the serpent, our enemy to this day—Satan. This is the first promise given of a Savior. In theological terms, this promise is referred to as the protoevangelion, the first mention of the good news of the gospel.

Fulfillment: John 1:14, 3:16, Romans 16:20, Galatians 4:4-5

The fulfillment of this verse is seen throughout the entire New Testament. We know Him today as Jesus Christ.

in your journal

☐ If you are creating an advent journal, write out the first promise of the world's Savior from Genesis 3:15. You can enclose it in a cloud or starburst to show this was a promise from God.

☐ Next, write out some of the fulfillment verses from John 1:14, 3:16, Romans 16:20 and Galatians 4:4-5. (Actually there are so many verses that show the fulfillment because this is Jesus! Messiah! The Anointed One!)

☐ Write out your thoughts about what this teaches you about God's sovereignty and His love.

☐ Write out any key words or things you'd like to reflect deeper on.

Come, Desire of Nations, come.
Fix in us Thy humble home.

Rise the woman's conquering Seed,
bruise in us the serpent's head.

Adam's likeness now efface,
Stamp Thine image in its place.

Second Adam from above,
Reinstate us in Thy love,

Hark, the herald angels sing,
glory to the newborn King!

-Hark! The Herald Angels Sing!

day two:

...all nations blessed

God's plan for a redeeming Savior wasn't haphazard or a random chain of events. It was specific in time, place, genealogy, and detailed exactly how and when it would happen. Nothing has ever changed that plan, and it is still at work today.

God is on the Throne!

And I will make you a great nation

CHRISTMAS CHALLENGE

To Do

Tonight take a break from all social media on every single device you have (log completely out so you don't mindlessly go to it) and use that time to make a list of things you want or need to do this season.

Even if you finish your list, do not log on again tonight. I promise everything can wait until tomorrow.

day two ...all nations blessed

Prophecies: to Abraham: Genesis 12: 3, 17: 7-8; To Isaac: 26: 2-4, To Jacob: Genesis 28: 14, Numbers 24: 17-19

These prophecies are called the Abrahamic prophecies by Bible scholars. They are given to Abram (Abraham) and his descendants, at a point where all the Biblical narrative narrows down to Abraham and his family. A promise was given to each descendant of each descendant, narrowing down the genealogy until Jesus' birth. Think of it as an address. Each line of an address on an envelope narrows it down, from the state, to the city, to the street, then the house, then the person. In the same way, God narrows down the family line to Jesus. You can almost sense the hope building, and the reminders over and over again that there is a plan, and God is in control.

Fulfillments: Matthew 1: 1, 17, Galatians 3: 16, Matthew 1: 2, Hebrews 11: 17-18, Luke 1: 31-33

Abraham received the promise from God first in Genesis 12:3, where God established His covenant with Abraham to give Him land, descendants, and blessing. Remember at this point, Abraham and Sarah were still without any children and were well beyond child-bearing age. Years had passed and Abraham still didn't have any children or see any of these great promises that God gave him fulfilled. His life had been hard, the wait had been very long, and in Genesis 15, Abraham calls out, frustrated, to God: *"O Lord God, what will you give me, for I continue childless, and the heir of my house is Eliezer of Damascus [his chief assistant and helper]?"*

So God reminds Abraham again in Genesis 17:7-8, right after He changes his name from Abram (exalted father) to Abraham (father of a multitude). At this point, Abraham and Sarah laughed because it was physically impossible for them to conceive. (Was this part of the reason God waited? Because He loves to be the God of the impossible?) But Abraham and Sarah DID conceive and have the son God had promised, Isaac. As the story unfolds, God also spoke to Isaac in Genesis 26:2-4. Then, in Numbers 24:17-19, a prophecy was told of the star of Jacob (Isaac's son), a scepter out of Israel, the Messiah.

in your journal

☐ Doodle Abraham and Isaac on your journal page and then write out the promise given to each man. Enclose the prophecies in a cloud since they came directly from God.

☐ As you are doodling or coloring your pages, reflect on God's timing and plan. Are there things you are tired of waiting for? Things you have given up hope for? Bring them all to God. Cultivate hope and thankfulness. God is the God of the impossible.

How silently, how silently
The wondrous gift is given!

So god imparts to human hearts
The blessings of His heaven.

No ear may hear His coming;
But in this world of sin,
Where meek souls will receive
Him still,
the dear Christ enters in.

-O Little Town of Bethlehem

day three

...a great Light

CHRISTMAS CHALLENGE

To Don't

This year don't be a freak.
Don't obsess about detail cleaning or getting the perfect decorations or preparing a beautiful meal.
Let the kids help.
Put up fewer decorations.
Eat frozen pizzas a night or two.

Tell your inner freak to chill because no one wants to be around a stressed out you. Enjoy the season, enjoy the process, be hospitable, make memories, enjoy the mess!

Our Savior and Messiah could have been anything: an adult (created like Adam, with one word from God), an angel, or a form we could never imagine. But instead God wanted the Messiah to be a helpless and weak human child, a child that would take on Himself the sins of the world.

day three ...a great Light

Prophecy: Isaiah 9:2-6

Today we're going to look at the first prophecy in our study from the prophet Isaiah. This prophecy was given to the kingdom of Judah (southern Israel) at a time when the nation of Assyria was coming to invade Judah and destroy them. Isaiah admits that there will be gloom and anguish, but they will also see a Great Light. Isaiah details this Light clearly in Isaiah 9:6.

The Light will be a Child. His humanity starts here. He has been —and always will be— God, but to be human, He had to be born. He knew what it was to live on earth, to be tempted, to suffer, and to live in this world fully understanding our struggle. How amazing it is that our God would make this child the way for us to return to Him.

This Light will be a Son, given. A male Savior given as a gift. No work on anyone's part. No striving or effort. Plainly and simply a gift, given to whoever will receive Him as Lord, Savior, and God. Fully human, fully divine as only the Messiah can be.

Fulfillment: Matthew 28: 18, John 1:1-5, John 8:12
1 Corinthians 15: 25-26

This prophecy also said the Child will have the government rest on His shoulder, and His name will be called Wonderful Counselor, Mighty God, Everlasting Father, Prince of Peace. He is in control of everything, always. Praise God that He knows every hair on our head, every sparrow of His creation, and that there is nothing that will happen to us that He does not know about and help us through.

in your journal

☐ Draw a baby in a manger with a bright starburst around Him and write out the first part of the prophecy.

☐ Draw a "bowling pin" Jesus and the symbol for government over one of His shoulders and a dove over the other.

☐ What does this prophecy and its fulfillment teach you about God?

Angels from the realms of glory,
Wing your flight o'er all the earth;
Ye who sang creation's story
Now proclaim Messiah's birth.
Come and worship,
come and worship,
Worship Christ,
the newborn King!

-Angels from the Realms of Glory

day four

born of a virgin...

Today we rejoice in the human side of Jesus Christ. He knows our joys, our fears, our temptations, our grief and our hopes. He was fully God, yet fully human. My mind can't comprehend the Creator of all as human, but I am so thankful He came to us in lowly human form to be that much closer to us. Holy infant so tender and mild.

CHRISTMAS CHALLENGE

To Do

Tonight put your feet up for a bit and look over the list you made a few days ago.

Go through the list and write down what you can delegate and to whom. Think through all options and delegate to kids, husband, bakeries (or Costco), paper plates, or your kids' friends. (Pay a teen from your church to wrap gifts!)

day four ...born of a virgin

Prophecy: Isaiah 7:14

There are a lot of Messianic prophecies in the Old Testament from the Prophet Isaiah. In fact, Isaiah had so many prophecies of the coming Messiah that he is often referred to as the fifth Evangelist, after Matthew, Mark, Luke, and John. The prophecy from Isaiah we'll look at today was given to Ahaz, an evil king of Judah, who was trusting in himself and his secret alliances while on the verge of war. God told Isaiah to meet Ahaz and tell him that the war would not happen, if Ahaz would trust in God. Isaiah told Ahaz that he could ask for a sign, but Ahaz refused, trusting more in his own alliances and plans, but acting like he revered God. In spite of this, God graciously gave Ahaz a sign through Isaiah: a son who would be born of a virgin.

Fulfillment: Matthew 1:18-23 and Luke 1:26-35

Some scholars say this is a dual prophecy both with a "here and now" part of the prophecy and a "not yet" aspect. They say the immediate context was fulfilled in Isaiah, when he married a virgin who conceived a son with Isaiah. His son had two names, one of which was Immanuel, God with us, named to be a reminder that God was with His people through troubling times; God would fulfill His promise of a Savior. The "here and now" would also include that when this child was old enough to know good from evil, the kings that Ahaz was afraid of would no longer be a threat. These parts of the prophecy were fulfilled in the days of Ahaz and Isaiah, but some important aspects of the prophecy were still to come in Jesus.

Yet other scholars say that this prophecy was only to have a single fulfillment in Christ. The single fulfillment idea points to the miraculous means God can use to fulfill His purposes, even an impossibility like that of a virgin birth. Either way, the inspired authors of the New Testament saw this prophecy clearly fulfilled in Christ, born of the virgin Mary.

> *"It is characteristic of predictive prophecy that it often mingles different times together in one composite picture."* -Alfred Martin

in your journal

- ☐ In your journal, draw Isaiah the prophet speaking to King Ahaz.
- ☐ Draw a speech bubble and write out Isaiah 7:14.
- ☐ What does this prophecy teach you about God? How can you praise Him for this?

Silent night, holy night,
all is calm, all is bright
round yon' virgin
mother and child.
Holy infant, so tender and mild,
sleep in heavenly peace,
sleep in heavenly peace.

-Silent Night

mighty God

day five

the throne of David

God chose king David's family to be the line which the Messiah would come from. God would preserve that line, despite the wars, terrors, and sinful failures of His people. His plan was and is unshakeable. He is able to do what He said He would do then, and now. Nothing is too difficult for Him.

CHRISTMAS CHALLENGE

To Do

Write in your calendar a time to bake a treat for a neighbor.

If you double the recipe you can also take a treat to the local homeless shelter, Sunday school teacher, fire station, or police station for some bonus points!

day five ...the throne of David

Another part of Isaiah's prophecy to the worried kingdom of Judah reaffirms the rule of the Messiah. This is the second part of the prophecy we looked at yesterday. Isaiah is repeating, reaffirming, and reassuring the Israelites that God will do what He has promised.

Prophecy: Isaiah 9: 7, Psalm 132: 11, Jeremiah 23: 5-6

Again, God is narrowing down the "address" of the Messiah. They not only had someone to look forward to as a ruler of peace, justice, and righteousness, but also to know that He would be on the throne of David. From David's royal family, or as the fulfillment puts it: " ...from the house and family of David." Even though the Messiah wouldn't come onto the scene for centuries, think of the hope these repeated promises must have given His people. God keeps reminding, keeps promising, and they just needed to remain hopeful in their waiting.

Fulfillment: Luke 1: 32-33, Luke 2: 4

I love how faithful God is in continually and lovingly reminding His people of the coming Messiah. His reminders were loving examples of His care. Almost all prophecies were given when the people were in tense or frightening situations. When their backs were up against the wall, or when all hope seemed lost, God lovingly took their eyes from their circumstances and lifted their faces up to Him as He reminded them that He has a plan, He is in control, and to trust in Him despite what the world looked like around them.

Look back at Isaiah 9:6. We touched on this earlier, but spend some time thinking again through all these wonderful names of the Messiah. Wonderful Counselor, Mighty God, Eternal Father, Prince of Peace. Write out what these titles mean to you and what they teach you about Jesus.

in your journal

☐ Draw a throne and scepter or crown.

☐ Draw Isaiah next to it, and write out his prophecy in a speech bubble, or just the second part of Isaiah 9:7.

☐ What aspect or truth about God does this prophecy and fulfillment demonstrate? How can you praise Him for that?

Here came the wise men from Orient land.
The King of kings lay thus in lowly manger.
In all our trials born to be our Friend!
He knows our need,
to our weakness is no stranger.

Behold your King; before Him lowly bend!
Behold your King; before Him lowly bend!

-O Holy Night

day six
born in Bethlehem

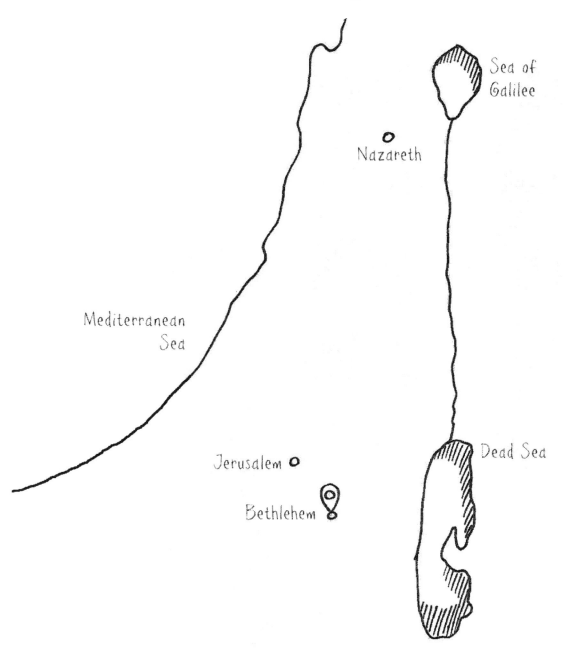

Sea of Galilee

Nazareth

Mediterranean Sea

Jerusalem

Bethlehem

Dead Sea

...being laid in a manger, He did, as it were, give an invitation to the most humble to come to Him. We might tremble to approach a throne, but we cannot fear to approach a manger. -C. H. Spurgeon

CHRISTMAS CHALLENGE

To Don't

Don't take on any extra projects for the rest of the year. I give you permission to say no. In fact, start practicing saying no to everything extra that comes your way unless you really feel called to do it. And even then, think for a day and bounce it off your family before you answer.

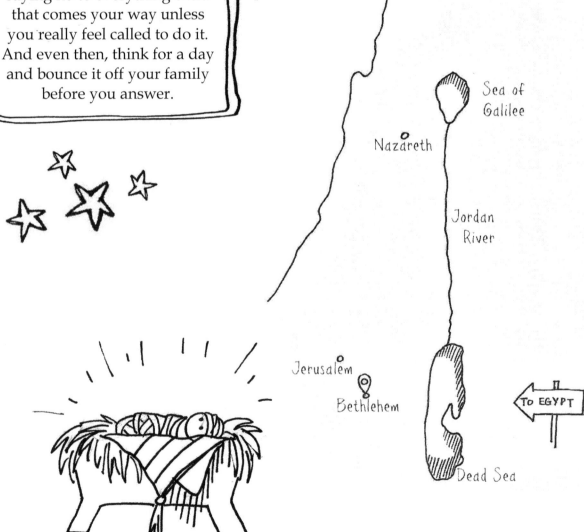

day six ...born in Bethlehem

Prophecy: Micah 5: 2-5

Today's prophecy comes from the Prophet Micah. He was a prophet to Judah during the reigns of several kings, including Ahaz, so he overlapped with Isaiah (who also prophesied to King Ahaz). Micah writes to Judah to warn them of the coming destruction and God's charges against them. When we get to our prophecy in chapter 5, Micah is warning them of Assyrian attack and the Ruler that will be born specifically in Bethlehem, the City of David, the King.

Fulfillment: Luke 2: 4-5, 15

The part that is so amazing about this prophecy, is not only that the prophet specifically named the city Messiah would be born in, but all that had to happen in Jesus' time to fulfill this prophecy. Mary, hugely pregnant and comfortable in her familiar hometown would not take on a trip like this unless she absolutely had to. And she wouldn't have had to, had Caesar Augustus not called a world wide census. And because he called a census, the tiny city they had to travel to was packed to overflowing with people, which meant no room was available for Joseph and Mary, even though she was going into labor.

Jesus was known to almost everyone as a carpenter from Nazareth (see John 7:41-42). The Jewish scholars knew that their Messiah would come from Bethlehem. They assumed that meant He would be born and raised in Bethlehem and start His rule from there, setting His people free from their oppressors. Many of them missed Him because He was not what they hoped for or expected. How many times in our own life do we miss seeing Jesus in the bigger picture because He isn't doing things as we want or expect Him to?

What does this teach you about Jesus? Why would the King of kings and Lord of lords and Creator of everything time His birth so that He would be born in an overflowing village and laid in an animal's feeding trough? What do you learn about God and His promise and plan for the Messiah?

in your journal

☐ Draw a map of the area of Bethlehem, Galilee, and Nazareth.

☐ Look back on your work so far. Take time to reflect on the truths you've learned. Is there a theme you're seeing in your notes about what this teaches you about God? Is He whispering something to you?

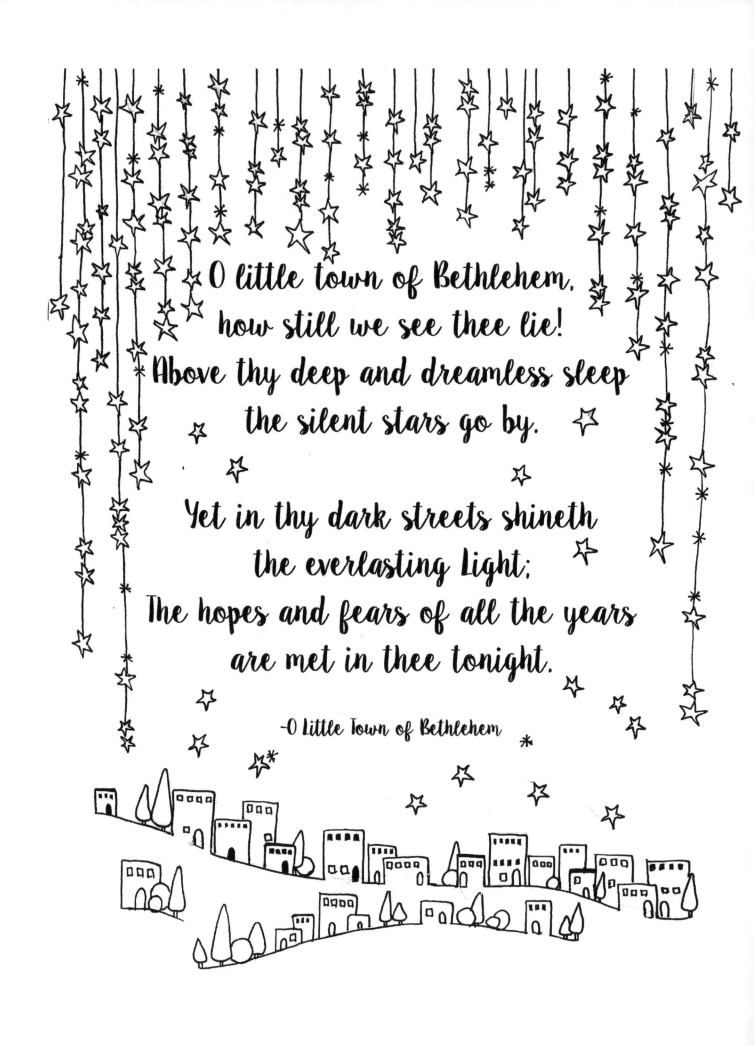

O little town of Bethlehem,
how still we see thee lie!
Above thy deep and dreamless sleep
the silent stars go by.

Yet in thy dark streets shineth
the everlasting Light;
The hopes and fears of all the years
are met in thee tonight.

-O Little Town of Bethlehem

day seven

...the magi

We should be glad of every thing that will show us the way to Christ. This star was sent to meet the wise men, and to conduct them into the presence chamber of the King . . .
–Matthew Henry

CHRISTMAS CHALLENGE

To Do

Find a good Christmas book to read this season. Stock a basket in the living room with great Christmas books for easy access!

Some favorites:

Skipping Christmas
—John Grisham

With kids:
The Lion, the Witch, and the Wardrobe —C.S. Lewis

The Best Christmas Pageant Ever
—Barbara Robinson

Polar Express-ChrisVanAllsburgh

How the Grinch Stole Christmas
—D. Seuss

day seven...the magi

Prophecy: Psalm 72: 5-11

Today's prophecy is one of the "now and not yet" prophecies of the Old Testament. It was a prophecy written by Solomon with a hint toward the eternal existence of Messiah. Read verses 5 and 7, paying close attention to the eternal references: while the sun endures, as long as the moon, till the moon be no more. Solomon was not eternal, so parts of this prophecy refer to the "not yet." Solomon is a "shadow" or "type" of Christ. Some parts refer to Solomon (the "now" parts of the section) and some refer to the Messiah (the "not yet" portions).

> *"That this prophecy must refer to the kingdom of the Messiah is plain, because there are many passages in it which cannot be applied to the reign of Solomon. There was indeed a great deal of righteousness and peace, at first, in the administration of his government; but, before the end of his reign, there were both trouble and unrighteousness. The kingdom here spoken of is to last as long as the sun, but Solomon's was soon extinct. Therefore even the Jewish expositors understand it of the kingdom of the Messiah. " -Matthew Henry*

Fulfillment: Matthew 2: 7-11

Re-read verse 10 of the prophecy. This was fulfilled both in Solomon's time (2 Chronicles 9:23-24) and in Christ's (Matthew 2:7-11). What I love about this prophecy is that the Magi (the wise men) knew and were expecting a king. They had been studying, learning, waiting, and finally—FINALLY—the Messiah had come! They came actively seeking Him (Matthew 2: 1-2). The Greek word for "saying" in verse 1 means "kept asking," giving the impression that they asked everyone they saw or met the question, over and over, excitedly trying to find the Messiah.

They also came fully prepared with gifts. There was no question in their minds that this prophecy would be fulfilled and they were ready to seek Him and give Him gifts that He fully deserved.

> *"...this shows that they were true seekers after God, because when He spoke to them, in whatever way it was, they heard and responded. Despite their paganism, quasi-science, and superstition they recognized God's voice when He spoke."*
> *-John MacAurthur*

in your journal

☐ In your journal, write out some of the gifts God has given you. They may be physical, spiritual, material, etc. Brainstorm for a few minutes then praise Him for each.

And by the light of that same star

Three wise men came from country far;

To seek for a king was their intent,

And to follow the star

wherever it went.

Noel, Noel, Noel, Noel,

Born is the King of Israel.

-The First Noel

day eight
the messenger

Don't waste the "waiting time" in your life. God builds beautiful, useful things in the person who redeems the waiting times.

CHRISTMAS CHALLENGE

To Don't

Don't stay up late tonight. Plan right now what time you should go to bed and start getting ready for bed about an hour before that.

Give yourself enough time to read a few pages of a Christmas book to your family (even teens!) and then read your own book quietly for a while.

day eight ...the messenger

Prophecy: Isaiah 40: 3-5, Malachi 3: 1

The Messiah will have an introduction to the world He is going to save. A messenger will be raised up before Christ, a voice calling out in the wilderness, one who will clear the way before the Savior. Obviously this was a time before printing presses, newspaper, or any modern form of communication. It was a time of scribes and hand-written information. Everything was word of mouth or stories passed down from generation to generation. God's plan provides a way for His Son to have maximum impact in a short time by preparing the way before He even comes into His public ministry.

Fulfillment: Matthew 3: 3, Mark 1: 3, Luke 3: 3-6, John 1: 23

The messenger is Christ's own cousin, John. John's back story is pretty amazing and if you have time today, take 15 minutes and read through the whole story in Luke 1-3. When John comes into the story, Luke says it was during the days of Herod (Luke 1:5) and Caesar Augustus (Luke 2:1) Which was a bad time for the Jewish people. There were massacres, cruelty, lies and brutality from the Roman government. And in the middle of all this darkness, God shines a bright light of hope and continues to fulfill His ultimate plan.

However, John lived in obscurity for most of his life. In Scripture we see his parents, his birth, and then nothing for decades. Waiting. Waiting and preparing for the promised Messiah. Zacharias and Elizabeth knew John was special and a gift of God. Zacharias even knew he was the prophet of the Most High (Luke 1:76). But during all this waiting, John was preparing. He was secretly learning, growing, and warming up because when he comes back on the scene, he KNOWS what he is doing. He is bold, brave, and speaks with no timidity (see Luke 3:7-9).

> "When it appears from earth that God is delaying, He is really putting pieces together that you had not thought of. He is engineering circumstances so that His power and glory will be on display. When God builds a waiting period into the course of our affairs, it means that what He is doing requires it! His apparent delays are loving, purposeful, and deliberate!"
> —Jennifer Kennedy Dean, "Live a Praying Life"

in your journal

☐ For this prophecy you could doodle any number of great scenes: Elizabeth and Zechariah and the angel, John rebuking the Pharisees, etc.

☐ Are you waiting for something in your life right now? How can you actively put to use this waiting time? Write out some things you could do to redeem the waiting time.

moses

jesus

day nine

...a prophet

Jesus is so much more than a prophet. Many, many people have missed the mark thinking Jesus was merely a prophet, or a good man, or a moral leader. He is Messiah, the final once for all sacrifice for our sins.

CHRISTMAS CHALLENGE

To Do
-

Reflect back over this year. Was there a major life event that happened, or a trial that God carried you through? As you reflect on your year, thank God for His faithfulness to you, then make or buy an ornament that will remind you of His faithfulness to you this year...to remind you for years to come.

day nine ...a prophet

Prophecy: Deuteronomy 18: 15-19

Today we go back to the time of Moses. The Israelites are about to enter their promised land after years and years of wandering in the desert. Moses is restating the Law that was given back in Exodus, to encourage them and remind this new generation of God's goodness and justice. While this is encouraging, it is also a sad time in Israel's history, a time when they asked that God never again speak directly to them… and from that moment on, God speaks through His prophets, Jesus being the mightiest "in deed and word in the sight of God and all the people." (Luke 24:19) Then Moses tells the Israelites what to look for in a prophet (Deut 18:20-22) The Israelites (and later the Jews) knew this to be the promise of a future prophet, a final prophet for Israel.

Fulfillment: John 1: 19-21, Matthew 21: 11, Luke 7: 16, 24: 19, John 6: 14, Acts 3: 18-22

When we look at John 1:19-21 we see the Jews sending priests and Levites from Jerusalem (these are the temple workers, the people who knew exactly who to look for and all about the Final Prophet they were expecting). They were sent to see if John the Baptist could be that prophet because of all the people he baptized and helped turn to God. Immediately John said "I am not the Messiah." In Matthew 21, the people call out that Jesus MUST be The Prophet. When Jesus raised the dead son, the people knew He was The Prophet of God. The common people knew that Jesus was a prophet, but the followers of Jesus knew He was The Prophet. In Acts 3:22, Peter directly states that The Prophet Moses was referring to is clearly and completely answered in Jesus Christ, the Messiah. The Jews, however, didn't want Jesus to be the Messiah. They were looking for a political ruler who would destroy Rome and end their oppression. Jesus instead was The Ruler making a way to end all oppression eternally. They wanted an earthly answer, He made an eternal one.

in your journal

☐ Draw Moses speaking to the Israelites from the mountain giving the prophecy.
or you could draw any of the fulfillments in their context:
or the palm leaves on the road from Matthew 21
or the loaves and fishes from feeding 5,000 in John 6.

☐ The Jews were looking for someone to change their current situation to a more comfortable one and missed the biggest plan of all. Are you caught up in situational problems that you want changed and missing God's bigger plan?

Truly He taught us to love one another;
His law is love and His Gospel is peace.

Chains shall He break
for the slave is our brother
And in His Name
all oppression shall cease.

Sweet hymns of joy
in grateful chorus raise we,
Let all within us
praise His holy Name!

-O Holy Night

day 10

...speaks in parables

"Do you know why Jesus taught in parables? It was a judgment on willful, hard-hearted unbelief... There is not another parable in the entire New Testament told by anyone but Jesus because parables are for judgment and only Jesus can render that judgment." -John MacArthur

CHRISTMAS CHALLENGE

To Do

Tonight write in a night on your calendar to go see Christmas lights!

When you head out, be sure to bring hot cocoa, tea, or coffee and Christmas music.

Extra Challenge:
Don't take any pictures or videos during the trip. See it all through your eyes, without a screen.

day 10 ...speak in parables

Prophecy: Psalm 78: 2, Isaiah 6: 9-10

Today's prophecy in Psalms was a song written to parents and grandparents. It reiterates the importance of telling history over and over to the next generation. Just as Deuteronomy 11:19 called the Israelites to do. So not only are the parents reminded to teach their children over and over the history and stories of their fathers, they themselves are reminded over and over to do it. As busy, sinful humans it is so easy to forget the wonderful things God has done for us. So not only is this prophecy a miracle of who the Messiah is, it is also a wonderful reminder of what we are called to do. Today's prophecy is one that was cited by Messiah Himself when His disciples asked Him why He spoke in parables.

Fulfillment: Matthew 13: 10-15, 34-35

Jesus spoke to the people in story form or in parables. Why? It's a fascinating topic to study, but I'll leave you with a few thoughts from wiser people than I. Either way, Jesus quotes these prophecies as fulfilled as does Matthew, who records it for us.

> "*Thus the parables spoke to the crowds do not simply convey information, nor mask it, but challenge the hearers.*"
> -D.A. Carson

> "*Jesus spoke in parables - earthly stories with a heavenly meaning. He did so that his disciples would comprehend his teachings and that unbelievers would be without comprehension. Those interested in understanding the truth of his message would understand while those not interested would remain without understanding.*" -Don Stewart

Jesus speaking in parables reinforces the truth that He is God. He knows everything and speaks in a way to bless and judge as only God can. Jesus taught people in a way to continue the story of God, God's story of a new covenant, a once for all sacrifice for sins, and a final redemption of His people for all time.

in your journal

☐ Doodle Jesus speaking to His disciples or you might look up some of the parables Jesus speaks in and doodle some of those:

Matthew 7:24-27

Mark 4:3-8

Mark 4:14-20

Luke 13:18-19.

Veil'd in flesh, the Godhead see;

Hail, the incarnate Deity:

Pleased, as man, with men to dwell,

Jesus, our Emmanuel!

Hark! the herald angels sing,

"Glory to the newborn King!"

-Hark! the herald angels sing

Color Break!

Wonderful

Counselor

Mighty God

Prince of Peace

day 11

...mounted on a donkey

"This entry into Jerusalem has been termed the triumph of Christ. It was indeed the triumph of humility over pride and worldly grandeur; of poverty over affluence; and of meekness and gentleness over rage and malice." -Adam Clarke

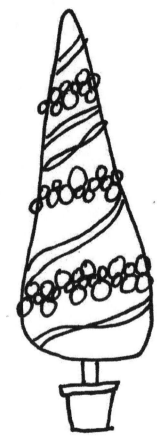

CHRISTMAS CHALLENGE

To Don't

Don't leave wrapping till the last minute. If you have gifts to wrap, take just 15 minutes each night to wrap a gift or two.

Leave yourself plenty of time as Christmas gets closer to enjoy the thrill of the season, not be bogged down wrapping!

day 11   ...humble, mounted on a donkey

Prophecy: Zechariah 9: 9-10, Psalm 118: 25-26

The prophet Zechariah was preaching to Judah after they returned from exile in Babylon. He was calling people to finish rebuilding the temple and to cleanse themselves and their land from sin. This prophecy was quoted by the New Testament authors as being fulfilled in Jesus when He entered Jerusalem, riding on the back of a donkey. Take special note of the qualities of the King that are listed in Zechariah.

Fulfillment: Matthew 21: 1-11, John 12: 12-16

In these verses the inspired authors recognized the prophecy in Zechariah as being fulfilled by Jesus when He entered into Jerusalem amidst singing and blessing and rejoicing. He came humbly, mounted on a mule. Not to make His journey easier, but to fulfill a prophecy in a way that the Jews would be sure to recognize but wouldn't cause a problem with Roman rulers. On the back of a donkey was how Solomon was made king all those years before when God promised David an heir to the throne that would rule forever. The Jews recognized this as another sign that Jesus really was the Messiah and from the correct lineage as promised.

D.A. Carson makes another interesting insight: *"Mark and Luke say the animal was so young that it had never been ridden. In the midst, then, of this excited crowd, an unbroken animal remains calm under the hands of the Messiah who controls nature."*

Now our study changes. Now we're entering into the final part of Messiah's life. Here we see the quietness identity of Jesus slowly being changed as He starts to more fully reveal Himself as the Messiah. But the most amazing thing is the perfect timing of this prophecy. As He rides in on a donkey, the timeline prophesied for the Messiah to appear in the prophecy of Daniel (which we won't study in this guide, but I highly recommend you read) is perfectly fulfilled. It could only be worked out so faultlessly by God.

in your journal

☐ Doodle palm branches to signify the triumphal entry into the city where Jesus would fulfill God's plan for salvation.

☐ Write out your thoughts above about why God would choose to reveal Himself this way. What does this teach you about Jesus?

Come, Thou long expected Jesus,
born to set Thy people free;
from our fears and sins release us,
let us find our rest in Thee.
Israel's strength and consolation,
hope of all the earth Thou art;
dear desire of every nation,
joy of every longing heart.

-Come, Thou Long Expected Jesus

day twelve

...the cornerstone

In this metaphorical description of Jesus Christ, He is called a stone, to denote His invincible strength and everlasting duration, and to teach His servants that He is their protection and security, the foundation on which they are built, and a rock of offence to all their enemies. He is the living stone, having eternal life in Himself, and being the prince of life to all His people. -Matthew Henry

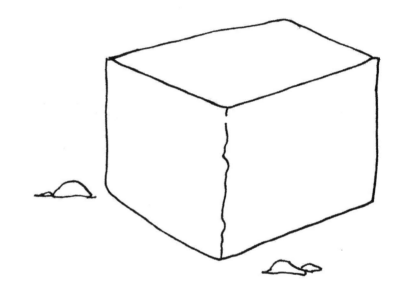

CHRISTMAS CHALLENGE

To Do

Decide on a special recipe you'd like to try. If you're anything like me, you've got zillions saved on Pinterest. Pull one up and try it.

-

Double the recipe to give one away.

day twelve   ...the cornerstone

Prophecy: Isaiah 28:16, Zechariah 10:4, Psalm 118:22

The prophet Isaiah spoke to the rulers of Jerusalem, who scoffed at God, who thought they had beaten death and Sheol and nothing could hurt them. God tells Isaiah to tell them that He will place a cornerstone as a foundation, and it isn't them. If you have time today, read through all of Isaiah 28 to get an idea of how the people were living, and the promise God makes to them. This cornerstone is precious, tested, and a sure foundation. In Zechariah, the prophet again narrows down where this cornerstone will come from. Pointing specifically to the lineage of Judah, and what He will ultimately be.

Fulfillment: Ephesians 2:19-22, 1 Peter 2:4-8, Acts 4:11

In Ephesians Paul is reminding them of who they are in Christ, all they have in Him, and then in verses 19-22 he gets to the fulfillment: Christ is the cornerstone, in whom the whole building is fitted together. The same is again stated by Peter in 1 Peter 2:4-8. Jesus Christ is the Chief Cornerstone and we are the living stones being built up from Him. He is a precious value to believers, but a stumbling stone and a rock of offense to those who don't believe. He is the stone which was rejected.

Here's a short definition of cornerstone from dictionary.com: the chief foundation on which something is constructed or developed.

The ISBE defines cornerstone as the foundation stone upon which the structure rested (Job 38:6; Isaiah 28:16; Jeremiah 51:26); or the topmost or cap-stone, which linked the last tier together (Psalms 118:22; Zechariah 4:7); in both cases it is an important keystone, and figurative of the Messiah, who is "the First and the Last."

in your journal

☐ Do a word study on cornerstone and what it means. Write out your notes or the definition.

☐ Without the cornerstone, the whole building would be weak. In what ways are you resting on your own ability instead of the cornerstone that keeps everything square and strong? Draw a cornerstone and write on it how you can make better use of His power and strength.

My hope is built on nothing less
Than Jesus blood and righteousness
I dare not trust the sweetest frame
But wholly trust in Jesus' name

Christ alone; Cornerstone
Weak made strong;
in the Savior's love
Through the storm,
He is Lord, Lord of all.

My Hope is Built on Nothing Less. Hillsong Music Publishing. 2011.

day 13

...rejected

men

rulers

brothers

"He was despised and rejected by men; a man of sorrows, and acquainted with grief ... Surely He has borne our griefs and carried our sorrows ..." -Isaiah 53

CHRISTMAS CHALLENGE

To Do

Today or this week, if you can, go through a drive through, coffee shop, or a restaurant and pay anonymously for someone's purchase.

Or, order pizza and tip the delivery driver extra big.

day thirteen ...rejected

Prophecy: Psalm 2: 1-2; 69: 9; 118: 22-23; Isaiah 53: 1-3

The pain and suffering of the Messiah starts in earnest in these prophecies and fulfillments. He knew exactly what the end of His life on earth would look like, and He knew all He would endure for the sake of saving the lost.

Fulfillment: Matthew 12: 14, John 7: 3-5, Matthew 21: 42-46, John 1: 10-11

Here we'll see a few of the many different ways Jesus was rejected. He was rejected by the rulers, His brothers, as a cornerstone, and by men. Today, look up the first prophecy, then immediately read the fulfillment of each. Work through each one this way.

1. Psalm 2:1-2 — Mathew 12:14 — rejected by rulers (read also Matthew 36:3-4, 47; Luke 23:11-12)
2. Psalm 69:9 — John 7:3-5 — rejected by family
3. Psalm 118:22-23 — Matthew 21:42-46 — rejected cornerstone (as we looked at yesterday)
4. Isaiah 53:1-3 — John 1:10-11 — rejected by men (see also John 12:37-38)

Looking back at these prophecies, I can't think of any more ways Jesus could have been rejected. Family, rulers, men, and then rejected for who He is. I know we all understand the pain of being rejected or ignored. It can stay with you a lifetime. Christ knew that He would be rejected by those very people He came to save, but He did it anyway. Scorned, despised, mocked, and rejected. It was worth it to Him.

Praise Jesus that He knew, endured, and rose above all of the pain of rejection so we could be together with Him in Heaven. Because of Christ's painful sacrifice and rejection, we will never be rejected by God. We see again God's great plan marching on as we look at the prophecies that were fulfilled toward the end of Jesus' life on earth.

in your journal

☐ In your journal you could draw a page with Christ or a cross in the center and all the people rejecting him around the outside. You could draw a rich, royal king with his hand up, in rejection.

☐ A simpler idea would be to draw the cross in the center of the page and then write the
☐ verses around the outside of it.

☐ Are there people in your life that have rejected Christ or you because of your witness for Christ? Make a list of them in your journal and keep praying for them.

God is not dead,
nor doth He sleep;
The wrong shall fail,
the right prevail,
With peace on earth,
good will to men.

-Henry Wadsworth Longfellow
"I Heard the Bells on Christmas Day"

day 14

...betrayed

Still, as of old,

man by himself is priced;

for thirty pieces Judas sold

himself, not Christ.

-English couplet

CHRISTMAS CHALLENGE

To Do

Tonight, or later this week, have dinner with only candle or lantern light with your best dishes and a table cloth.

It doesn't have to be a fancy meal. Leftovers, corndogs, or simple foods taste amazing served fancy!

day fourteen ...betrayed

Prophecy: Psalm 41: 9, Zechariah 11: 12

David was a "type" of Christ as the King of Israel. In many of his psalms, David writes songs detailing his struggles and sufferings which also foreshadowed many of the same sufferings that Christ would go through to fulfill God's plan to make a way back to Him.

The prophecy cited in Zechariah is amazing in how specific it is when matched up to the fulfillment in Matthew.

Fulfillment: Matthew 26: 14-16, Mark 14: 10-11; 44-46
Luke 22: 3-7; 47-48

Judas, friend, disciple, confidant, betrayed Jesus. He walked with Him, talked with Him, worked with Him, yet still betrayed Him. And it wasn't merely Judas taking advantage of something that happened to pop up, Judas bargained and negotiated, willing to work with those who wanted to kill Jesus to get the best deal for himself (Matthew 26:15).

> *"The gaping chasm between a public persona and a private self — what may be called a double life — always begins as a tiny crack, a decision to conceal sin. Sin abhors the light of truth; it demands secrecy of the sinner."* -Charles Swindoll

Lots of theologians have speculated about Judas' reasons, and there is probably more than one right answer to it all. But, it does make me want to pause here and take stock of my own inner spiritual situation. Am I in a prideful, arrogant, greedy place in my own life that I will deliberately ignore or betray Christ or conceal sin? Every single failure in life starts with a tiny step, repeated over and over. Rarely is it one giant leap into sin.

> *"Do you mortify; Do you make it your daily work; be always at it while you live; cease not a day from this work; be killing sin or it will be killing you."* -John Owen

in your journal

☐ Draw Judas holding a stack of coins or a bag of money.

☐ Self-observation, or heart-keeping, is crucial to a well lived Christian life. How are you doing on keeping your heart and mortifying sin? Heart-keeping is searching the Word, then searching your own heart. Take a few minutes today to search your heart through searching the Scriptures.

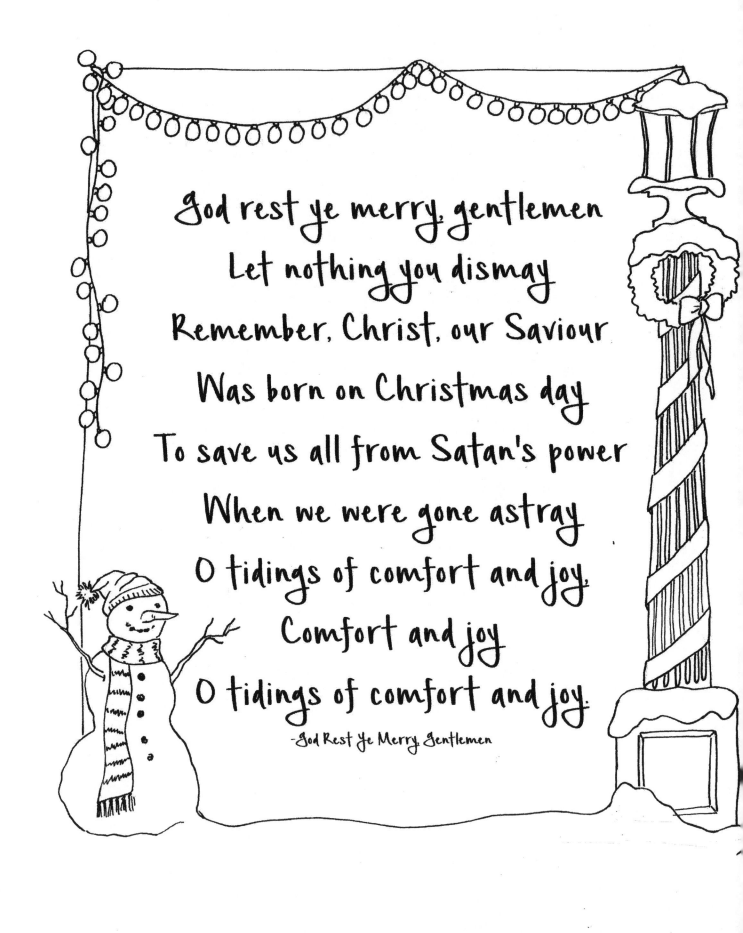

God rest ye merry, gentlemen
Let nothing you dismay
Remember, Christ, our Saviour
Was born on Christmas day
To save us all from Satan's power
When we were gone astray
O tidings of comfort and joy,
Comfort and joy
O tidings of comfort and joy.

-God Rest Ye Merry, Gentlemen

day 15

...30 pieces of silver

"Judas perpetrated his dirty deed by meeting with the leaders of Israel and bargaining for thirty pieces of silver, something around twenty to twenty-five dollars." -John MacArthur

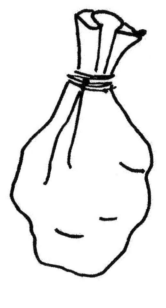

CHRISTMAS CHALLENGE

To Don't

Don't let simple Christmas traditions be overlooked this year. If you have a tradition you haven't done in a while, be sure to make time for it this year.

Some fun ones we've occasionally forgotten:
A breakfast of homemade cinnamon rolls

Snowman pancakes with chocolate chip eyes and smile and bacon scarf

Hiding a special ornament in the tree
(or in my husband's case, a 12" GI Joe sniper in full ghillie suit).

.day fifteen ..30 pieces of silver

Prophecy: Zechariah 11: 12-13

Let's look a little closer into the price Judas received for turning Jesus over to the Roman authorities and this whole amazing prophecy in Zechariah. When you read the prophecy, it reads exactly like the scene that takes place with Judas and the chief priests in Matthew 26:14-16. But back when it was written is was the price a man would receive for a slave.

Fulfillment: Matthew 26: 14-16, Luke 22: 3-6

We need to trace these 30 pieces of silver all the way through what they brought about for Judas. First, we see Judas bargaining for the price, and it is settled to buy Judas' service to turn Christ over to them for the price of 30 pieces of silver. Then, as the prophecy says, "throw it to the potter," Judas feels remorse for his betrayal and throws the money back to the chief priests (Matthew 27:3-10) who then use it to buy a potter's field, the Field of Blood.

If you follow Judas in the book of Acts you'll see that in Peter's exhortation he spoke of Judas' end. "Brethren, the Scripture had to be fulfilled, which the Holy Spirit foretold by the mouth of David concerning Judas, who became a guide to those who arrested Jesus. For he was counted among us, and received his portion in this ministry. (Now this man acquired a field with the price of his wickedness; and falling headlong, he burst open in the middle and all his bowels gushed out. And it became known to all who were living in Jerusalem; so that in their own language that field was called Hakeldama, that is, Field of Blood.)" --Acts 1:16-19

Take special note, again of all the prophecy fulfilled here. Just in the price of silver, the betrayal, and the field, there are too many for this to be a coincidence, and they are impossible to force to happen. God wants to show us that He alone knows the future, He alone has a plan, and He alone is capable of seeing it through to the end He already knows. This Christmas, rest in the God of prophecy, the God of the future, the God who knows.

in your journal

- ☐ In your journal you might want to draw a stack of coins or a money bag and write out the prophecy and fulfillment verses.
- ☐ Write out Isaiah 14:27.
- ☐ What concerns or worries can you give to God this season? Write them out and pray through them.

A King like this, a saving
Love that would not forsake us
Betrayed by a kiss and led
To the cross for our forgiveness
The Light, the Light has come
He is Christ, the Lord
He is Christ, our Savior
I bow my heart
before no other name,
I bow my heart
before no other King.

Chris Tomlin. A King Like This. Adore: Christmas Songs of Worship.
Capitol Christian Music. 2015.

day 16

...tried and condemned

"More than 700 years before Jesus was born, Isaiah wrote a description of the future sufferings of the Messiah…"
-Tim LaHaye, Jesus, Who is He?

CHRISTMAS CHALLENGE

To Do

Before the season is over, plan to sleep out by your tree one night (or let your kids camp out there). Make it a fun night by watching your favorite Christmas movie and having a special treat.

day sixteen ...tried and condemned

Prophecy: Isaiah 53: 8

Isaiah 53 is probably the most famous prophetic chapter in the Old Testament. It is so vivid in detail it seems as if Isaiah was standing there during Jesus' final days of life on this earth. For these final sections we'll be spending quite a bit of time in Isaiah 53. Each day I'd like you to read through Isaiah 53. It's just 12 verses but so amazing in its message and how closely it parallels Jesus' life.

> *"That this chapter does indeed concern Messianic fulfillment can be seen in many Hebrew synagogues, where one chapter of Isaiah is read aloud every Sabbath day, they habitually skip chapter 53. Why? Because the parallels in this prophecy are so close to some of the events in the life of Jesus Christ that it is hard to explain why they rejected Him. Consequently, they think it wisest to ignore the chapter."*
> -Tim LaHaye

Fulfillment: Matthew 27: 1-2, Mark 15: 1-2, Luke 22: 66-23: 4, John 18: 33-40

Yesterday we saw Judas' betrayal and Jesus' arrest at night, under the cover of darkness. Early in the morning, Jesus was brought before Pilate, the Roman governor. The Jews were living under the rule of Rome and they hated it. The Roman rulers took away the Jew's power to convict an offender with the death penalty, so they brought Jesus to Pilate to issue the penalty for them. Pay special attention to how Jesus behaved during His arrest and trial. He knew the Father's plan. He humbled Himself and became obedient to death, even death on a cross—which He knows is coming.

> *"The nighttime capture at Gethsemane initiated a series of six trials; three before the Jewish religious authorities and three before the civil authorities of Rome. As we shall see, all were illegal. And unlike most trials, these did not make the pursuit of truth their primary object."* -Charles Swindoll

Today take some time to praise Him for loving you so much He went through these completely illegal trials for you. You were on His mind. You were His goal.

in your journal

☐ Read through Isaiah 53 and write out any verses that stand out to you.

☐ In your journal you might want to draw a courtroom gavel or Jesus before Pontius Pilate and/or write out the prophecy verse above.

☐ What does this teach you about God?

Then let us all with one accord
Sing praises to our heavenly Lord,
That hath made heaven
and earth of naught,
And with His blood
mankind hath bought.
Noel, Noel
Noel, Noel!
Born is the King of Israel!

-The First Noel

day 17
...silent

For it was evident to Him (Jesus) that Pilate knew He was innocent and wanted to deliver Him and was seeking some way to do so. If He had replied to Pilate in any way, the governor would have used His words to dismiss the charge and free Him immediately.

-Ray Steadman

CHRISTMAS CHALLENGE

To Do

Buy a bottle of sparkling grape juice or sparkling apple cider and save it to serve with a very simple dinner of appetizers or finger foods. If you have fancy glasses, be sure to break them out and toast each other at your dinner.

day seventeen ...silent

Prophecy: Isaiah 53: 7-8

There are so many prophecies in Isaiah 53 that obviously point to Christ! In this prophecy we see the Messiah being oppressed, afflicted, and led to His death, but He remains silent. What kind of Messiah is this? We see that the Messiah will be innocent like a lamb, yet led away to His slaughter, and stricken for the transgressions of others.

Fulfillment: Matthew 27: 12-14

Pilate, the governor or Rome, was stuck between a rock and a hard place. He didn't want a Jewish revolt, but he also didn't want to accuse a man who was innocent either. Pilate had already made several big mistakes during his time as a governor, and he was worried about another revolt or riot destroying his rule. At this point in the Messiah's story, the crowds had already made their choice, Jesus had already plainly answered Pilate's earlier questions, and there was nothing left to say. So rather than defend Himself or say anything to prove His innocence, He chose to remain silent.

All of these trials were an unjust mockery of the law. Illegal proceedings, false accusations, and everything that could go wrong from our human viewpoint. But they were also part of God's great plan of salvation, and Jesus, the Messiah, was willing to endure the lies, beatings, mockeries, and proceedings so He could bring us back to Him. The suffering Servant was silent to fulfill prophecy and ultimately fulfill the greatest plan of all.

in your journal

☐ Read through Isaiah 53 and turn it into a time to praise Him for all He suffered for you.

☐ Draw a lamb and write out the verses.

What can I give Him,

poor as I am?

If I were a shepherd,

I would bring a lamb:

If I were a wise man,

I would do my part;

Yet what I can give Him:

give my heart.

-In the Bleak Midwinter

day 18
smitten, mocked

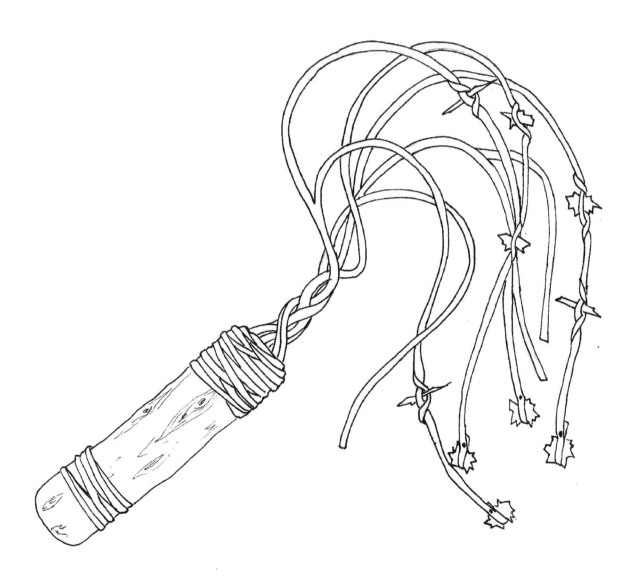

The Servant chose His sufferings willingly and He moves forward with resolute determination, confident in God's overruling help.

-ESV Study Bible

CHRISTMAS CHALLENGE

To Do

As you get Christmas cards, letters, and emails from friends and family, take deliberate time each day to read through them and pray for each of the senders. -

day eighteen ...smitten, mocked

Prophecy: Micah 5: 1, Isaiah 50: 6-7; 52:13-15

The first part of Micah 5 describes the new Shepherd King for Israel and gives His birthplace and predicts some of His sufferings (Micah 5:1b). He will be struck by a rod, and He is the judge of Israel. In Isaiah we also see Him being struck. Rods were typically used for criminals or fools, so this would be a very different Shepherd King than what Israel wanted. They wanted relief from Roman rule, not a King who would be beaten and mocked.

Fulfillment: Matthew 26: 67-68, Matthew 27: 27-30, Matthew 27: 39-44

Jesus was not only physically beaten, bruised, and whipped, but also mentally and emotionally mocked, taunted and abused. He did it willingly. The Shepherd King of Israel—Messiah, Savior of all mankind—treated worse than a criminal or a fool. He entered into Jerusalem highly exalted and praised, and just a few days later his appearance was "disfigured beyond that of any man and His form marred beyond human likeness." Re-read the prophecy in Isaiah 50:6. He OFFERED His back, He did not hide His face from the mocking and spitting. If He endured this all for you, what does it teach you about God's plan and Jesus, the suffering Servant?

in your journal

☐ Read through Isaiah 53.

☐ Write out Isaiah 52:13 –53:2

☐ What does this tell you about Jesus?

Why lies He in such mean estate,

Where ox and ass are feeding?

Good Christians, fear, for sinners here

The silent Word is pleading.

Nails, spears shall pierce him through,

the cross he bore for me, for you.

Hail, hail the Word made flesh,

the Babe, the Son of Mary.

-What Child is This?

day 19

...died in pain and suffering

Believer, come near the cross today, and humbly adore the King of glory as having once been brought far lower, in mental distress and inward anguish, than any one among us; and mark his fitness to become a faithful High Priest. -C.H. Spurgeon

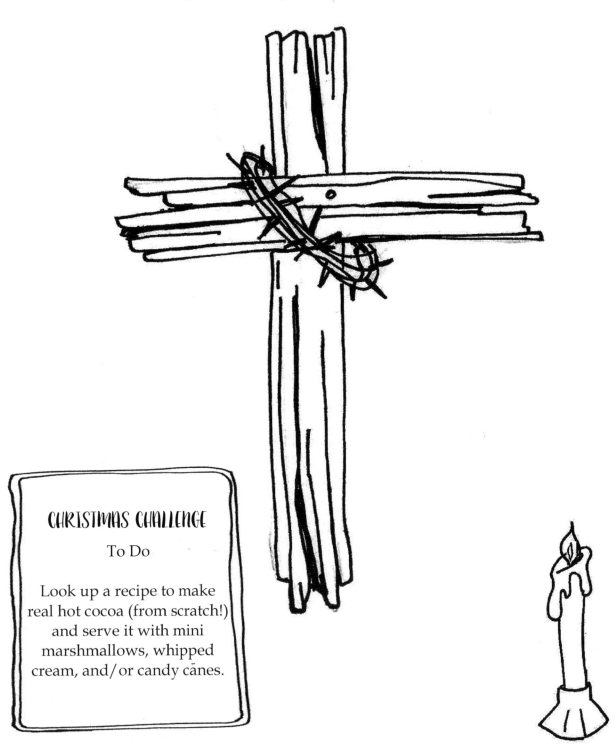

CHRISTMAS CHALLENGE

To Do

Look up a recipe to make real hot cocoa (from scratch!) and serve it with mini marshmallows, whipped cream, and/or candy canes.

day 19 ...died in pain and suffering

Prophecy: Psalm 22: 1, 14-16

Psalm 22 was a prayer written by David as he suffered under attacks of enemies. David was innocent, yet was not delivered from the anguish of vicious onslaughts of others. No other psalm follows as close as this to the crucifixion of Jesus on the cross. Jesus quoted Psalm 22:1 while hanging on the cross, and Matthew and John both quote from it in their accounts of the final days of Christ's life on earth.

Fulfillment: Matthew 27: 31-38, Mark 15: 22-24, John 19: 23-24

There was so much fulfilled in the prophecies by the horrible crucifixion and death of Jesus, the Messiah. God requires absolute holiness and knew our need of a permanent Savior. A Messiah to save His people from their sins forever. Christ lived the perfect life, and was the perfect, spotless, unblemished sacrifice for our sins. He alone is worthy. He was willing to suffer the anguish of crucifixion for you.

> *"Our Lord's suffering in this particular form was appropriate and necessary. It would not have sufficed for our Lord merely to have been pained in body, nor even to have been grieved in mind in other ways: He must suffer in this particular way. He must feel forsaken of God, because this is the necessary consequence of sin. For a man to be forsaken of God is the penalty which naturally and inevitably follows upon his breaking his relation with God."* -C.H. Spurgeon

If you have time today, look at the other prophecies fulfilled on this day in Christ's life:

Prayed for persecutors
Isaiah 53:12 — Luke 23:34

Forsaken
Psalm 22:1 — Matthew 27:46

Committed Himself to God
Psalm 31:5 — Luke 23:46

Given gall and vinegar
Psalm 69:21 — John 19:28-29

You might want to draw a big cross on your page and write out all the prophecies and fulfillments of Christ on the cross, listed above. Make it a simple but meaningful page in your journal.

in your journal

☐ Read through Isaiah 53.

☐ Write out Isaiah 53:7-8.

You shone upon the Earth
but who will understand?
You came unto Your own
but who will recognize?
Your birth was prophesied,
for You were the Messiah
Who came and walked upon the Earth.

Matt Redman. Light of the world. Glory in the Hightst. Thank You Music. 2000

day 20

cast lots, suffer with sinners

"And again we see not a humiliated Christ dying with criminals, but an exalted Christ fulfilling prophecy."
-John MacArthur

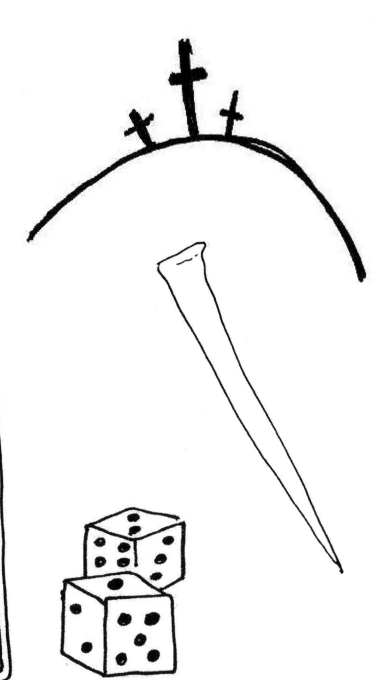

CHRISTMAS CHALLENGE

To Do

More Christmas Books to read:

Mr. Willowby's Christmas Tree
-Robert Barry

Christmas Cookie Sprinkle
Snitcher
-Robert Krauss

The Christmas Miracle of Jonathan
Toomey
-Susan Wojchiechowski

day twenty... cast lots, suffer with sinners

Prophecy: Psalm 22: 1, 18, Isaiah 53: 12

Today we're still in Psalm 22, the psalm of an anguished David. Remember that David is a type of Christ, meaning some aspects of David's life foreshadowed or were a picture of the life or work of Christ. In these two prophecies we see David foreshadow the garments being divided up and lots being cast for them. And in Isaiah 53 we see a prophecy of spoils divided among the strong.

Fulfillment: Matthew 27: 35, Mark 15: 27-28, Luke 23: 33, John 19: 23-24

As we get further into the prophecies of Christ, I am so amazed at how many are perfectly fulfilled in Christ's life and death. That people would cast lots for His clothes and divide up the "spoils" reassures us that Christ is indeed the Messiah. These are things that only God could know beforehand. Christ walked the path God had laid out for Him before the foundation of the world. He is a God who loves, pursues, and even dies for that relationship. We should be filled with hope and assurance because God KNOWS. He knows our sorrow, our joys, and our struggles. He had a good and perfect plan for Christ's life and a good and perfect plan for our life.

> *"He bore the sinner's sin, and he had to be treated, therefore, as though he were a sinner, though sinner he could never be. With his own full consent he suffered as though he had committed the transgressions which were laid on him. Our sin, and his taking it upon himself, is the answer to the question, 'Why hast thou forsaken me?'"* -C.H. Spurgeon

in your journal

☐ Read through Isaiah 53.

☐ Write out Isaiah 53:3-4.

☐ Some ideas for your page might include a pair of dice rolled for Jesus' clothes or a drawing of the three crosses, signifying He was crucified beside sinners.

Chains shall He break
for the slave is our brother
And in His name
all oppression shall cease
Sweet hymns of joy
in grateful chorus raise we.
Let all within us
praise His holy name.
-O Holy Night

day 21

no bones broken

Because the passion of Christ took place the week of Passover, the early church quickly understood that Jesus fulfilled the symbolism in the Passover meal as "the Lamb of God, who takes away the sin of the world!" The marking of blood on the doorposts has a clear tie to the shedding of Jesus' blood on the cross, and it is therefore no surprise to see the Lord's disciples link His death to the Passover throughout their writings. -www.ligonier.org

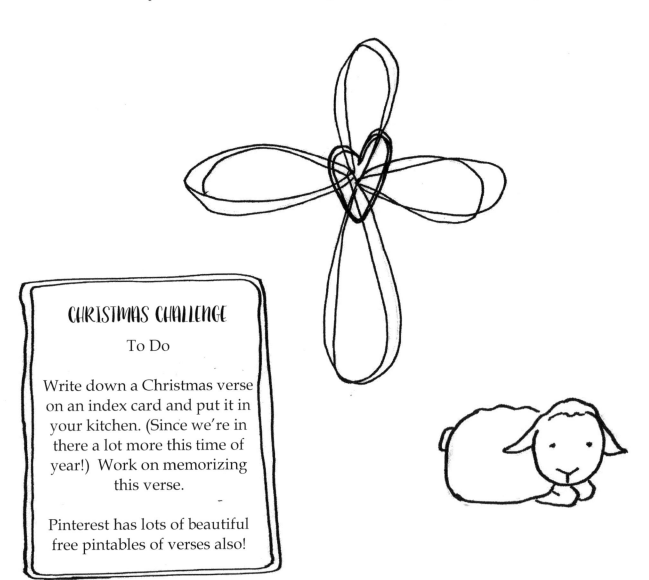

CHRISTMAS CHALLENGE

To Do

Write down a Christmas verse on an index card and put it in your kitchen. (Since we're in there a lot more this time of year!) Work on memorizing this verse.

Pinterest has lots of beautiful free pintables of verses also!

day twenty one ...no bones broken

Prophecy: Numbers 9: 12, Psalm 22: 17, Psalm 34:20

This prophecy is fascinating and dates back to Moses and the Israelites when they were setting up the sacrificial system of the tabernacle. The tabernacle was a type of Christ, as were the sacrificial animals used to cover the guilt of sin. All of them pointed forward to the final, once and for all sacrifice of Christ, our Passover (1 Corinthians 5:7) . Take special note of the specific way they were to care for the Passover lamb, not left until morning, and not breaking any of its bones. Why was this so important? Perhaps to point the Jews and anyone else who knew these rules that Christ is our ultimate Passover sacrifice.

Fulfillment: John 19: 31-37

I've often wondered how Christ could be crucified and have no bones broken in the process. I've done some research and come to a conclusion that I'll present here so you can make your own decision. First, we know the Romans crucified Him by pounding nails through his hands and feet. How did they hammer in big nails without breaking His bones? Some researchers and doctors have suggested that they didn't hammer into his hands, as many traditional paintings show, but that they went through the wrist, where the ulna and radius meet. The Greek word for hands is "cheir" and was used by Thomas in John 20:25 and in Acts 12:7 where the chains fall from Peter's "cheir," or hands. The Greeks had no word for wrists, so anything in that area would be referred to as hands. No one chains up the hands, but rather the wrists. And this also makes sense for how the whole weight of a hanging body could be supported. Nails through the hands would just tear through the small bones and ligaments there, but through the wrists would give much more stability. Also the nails through the feet could have been easily driven through the large metatarsals, or there has been some findings where maybe they also nailed between the Achilles' tendon and the rest of the foot.

Thus, it is very feasible to think of Jesus being nailed to a cross and have no bones broken. Prophecy was being fulfilled by men who had no idea that they were doing it as they were crucifying the Messiah who died for them.

in your journal

☐ Read through Isaiah 53.

☐ Write out Isaiah 53:5-6.

☐ Your journal page might draw a lamb with the verses written near it.

Mary did you know

that your baby boy will some day walk on water?

Mary did you know

that your baby boy will save our sons and daughters?

Did you know that your baby boy has come to make

you new?

This child that you've delivered, will soon deliver you.

-Mary Did You Know?

day 22
satisfied to die
as a sin offering

"God says: Here is my Only Begotten Son, my other self; He takes on Himself the nature of these rebellions creatures, and He consents that I should lay on Him the load of their iniquity, and visit in His person the offences which might have been punished in the persons of all these multitudes of men: and I will have it so."

-C.H. Spurgeon

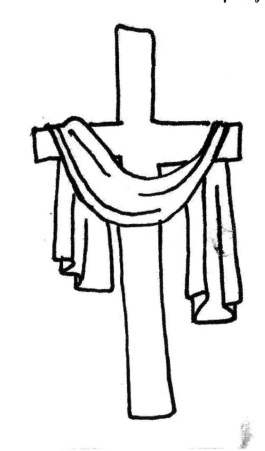

CHRISTMAS CHALLENGE

To Do

This season, try to find a restful spot for yourself. It might be a secluded park or nearby trail, or it might be a cozy nook set up in your house, or a neighborhood coffee shop. Be deliberate about going there soon, right smack dab in the middle of the hectic Christmas season, for a quiet break.

Make it a habit to return to your spot often. Schedule times for yourself into your week or month to deliberately visit this spot to rest, think, and spend time alone with God.

day twenty two ...satisfied to die as a sin offering

Prophecy: Isaiah 53: 5-6, 8, 10-12

"God doesn't choose to come with power and might and warfare to wipe men off the face of the earth . . . God's method is to break through man's rebelliousness not by might, not by power---but by love, by love that suffers. And when he does, and the heart responds by opening up, then all the majesty and the power of God are poured into that life to bring to it the fulfillment that God has intended for human hearts." -Ray Stedman

Fulfillment: John 12: 27-33; 18: 37, Galatians 3: 13-14, Hebrews 12: 2-3, Romans 4:24-25, 2 Corinthians 5:21

I love the imagery I heard from a sermon a while ago. Think of John the Baptist when he baptized Jesus and imagine that as John is baptizing all the people came with labels on their forehead. A label that stateed their sins, what they were carrying on themselves. And as they each got baptized their label washes off and floats on top of the water where they were. Jesus then comes in to get baptized but since He is sinless He doesn't carry a label on Himself. Instead all the labels are floating around Him and He says He'll take each one of those and stick them on Him. Then He takes them with Him to the cross and leaves them there (Colossians 2:14). He cancels out the debt forever. It's ALL His work. There is nothing we could ever do other than accept what He did on our behalf. If we had to do something in addition to what He did, His work wouldn't have been enough and He would have died in vain. (Galatians 2:21)

"Dear friends, are you living by faith upon the Son of God? Are you trusting in God? Are you believing His promises? Some think that this is a very little thing, but God does not think so. Faith is a better index of character than anything else. The man who trusts his God, and believes His promises, is honoring God far more than is the man who supposes that by any of his own doings he can merit divine approval and favor." -C. H. Spurgeon

in your journal

☐ Write out Isaiah 53:7-8.

☐ Your journal page might have a lamb with the verses written near it.

☐ Again, check your heart. Are you living a life that is working for some aspect of your salvation? Are you trying to fulfill a list of do's and don'ts? Christ died once for all. And because of His death, God was completely satisfied to forgive us our sins. There is nothing you can do to make your salvation "stronger" or eternal life "more secure." It was secured for believers before the beginning of time. (2 Timothy 1:9) Our holy living should be only in thanksgiving and love for Him, not in trying to earn something He already gave to us. Praise God He made a way!

What a wonderful, wonderful Savior,

Who would die on the cross for me!

Freely shedding His precious lifeblood,

That the sinner might be made free.

-Frederick A. Graves

day 23

...buried in a rich man's tomb

Joseph (of Arimathea) was committed to a Man who was dead and not yet risen. He was so convinced that Jesus was who He claimed to be, Joseph stepped out in faith and courageously gave Him the dignified burial He deserved.   -John MacArthur

CHRISTMAS CHALLENGE

To NOT do

Don't think you have to fit it all in this Christmas season. Intentionally schedule a party or potluck get together AFTER the season.

Gather your friends in the slower time in January or February and extend the season! No one will feel the pressure to bring gifts!

day twenty three   ...buried in a rich man's tomb

Prophecy: Isaiah 53: 9

Some people say that the prophecies that are answered in Jesus could have been staged by a man who wasn't really Messiah. Jesus could have ridden into Jerusalem on a donkey because He was trying to fulfill prophecy, He could have done any number of things to try to fulfill prophecy. But this and many others (specific place of birth, specific time of birth, specific things the Roman soldiers would do, and this, happening after His death) He had absolutely no control over. If any normal man had tried to fulfill Messianic prophecy, no one could have fulfilled all as Christ did.

Fulfillment: Matthew 27: 57-61, Mark 15: 42-47, Luke 23: 50-56, John 19: 38-42

Joseph of Arimathea, a rich man who followed Jesus, had the courage to ask for Jesus' body from Pilate. It was getting late in the day, the horror of crucifixion was over, all the men were dead, and since it was the day before Sabbath, preparations had to be made now. The Sabbath had very specific rules that the Jews strived to keep, and since preparing and burying the body of Jesus would be considered work, and therefore a break of the rules of Sabbath rest, Joseph bravely asked to take care of Jesus' body.

Most criminals that were crucified on a cross were not given a proper burial, but Joseph, together with a few other disciples asked to take care of His body properly. Since it was evening and there wasn't much time left before Sabbath, they placed him in a tomb they had access to, Joseph of Arimathea's own tomb. It worked, it made sense, and it was all they could do with the time they had before Sabbath. I doubt if they even thought through the prophecy of Isaiah, given hundreds of years earlier, that the Messiah would be buried with the rich. They were just doing what they could, with what they had, as well as they could in their grief-stricken state.

in your journal

☐ Write out Isaiah 53:9-10.

☐ Joseph and the other followers of Christ were doing what they could with what they had and God used them, even in their grief, sorrow, and confusion. If He could do that then, He can definitely do it today.

Hallelujah, we've been found!

A child is born to save us now. Jesus!

Hallelujah, light has come!

A Savior who will set us free.

A promise for those who believe.

-Hallelujah (Light has Come). Barlow Girl.

He is alive

day 24

Anyone knowledgeable about the Christian faith is aware of the significance of the cross, where our sins were borne by the Lord Jesus Christ to free us from the penalty and guilt of sin. Just as significant is the resurrection of Jesus Christ—the single greatest miracle the world will ever know. It demonstrates Christ's finished work of redemption and reminds us that His power over death will bring us to glory.   -John MacArthur

CHRISTMAS CHALLENGE

To Do

Make that hot cocoa
or get a coffee,
take a book,
go to that quiet spot,
and
Praise God that
He is RISEN!

Day twenty four ...He is ALIVE!

Prophecy: Psalm 16: 10-11; 24: 7-10; 30: 3, 110: 1

The Messiah will not remain dead! He will be restored to life and raised again. Then He will sit at God's right hand, His enemies will be his footstool, and He will enter through the gates into Heaven!

Fulfillment: Matthew 28: 5-7, Mark 16: 19, Luke 24: 5-53, Acts 1: 6-11

Jesus. Messiah. Savior.

He came to live. To grow. To be tested. To feel the searing pain of betrayal, mocking, beating. He came to serve, to bless, to divide. The Savior, Jesus Christ, the Messiah. He is the One we worship! He is who we celebrate tomorrow and forever! And the best part? His story is not over! It doesn't end here! There are yet more prophecies about the rest of His life that He continues to live even now in Heaven!

He is coming back!

He will make things right!

He will end all pain and suffering!

He will at last completely crush and destroy the snake forever!

Praise God for His Son!

in your journal

☐ Write out Isaiah 53:11-12.

☐ What do these prophecies and their fulfillments teach you about God?

☐ In your journal, write down your thoughts and write out a prayer to God thanking Him for His good and gracious gift of the Messiah, Jesus Christ.

☐ Doodle some gift boxes and write on them some of the prophecies that have been especially meaningful to you.

Good Christian men, rejoice,

with heart and soul and voice;

Now ye need not fear the grave:

Peace! Peace!

Jesus Christ was born to save!

Calls you one and calls you all,

to gain His everlasting hall.

Christ was born to save!

Christ was born to save!

-Good Christian Men Rejoice

...to be continued!

The best news? The story doesn't end here!
There is SO MUCH more!

Those of you who are suffering, it is temporary!

Those of who you who are grieving this season,
some day it will be turned into rejoicing.

Those of you who are hurt, betrayed, alone,
lean into your Messiah.

He has done ALL He said He would do.

He will continue to fulfill His promises.

Nothing, even impossible odds, will stop God
from doing what He intends to do.
Nothing.

Sinful men, who nailed Jesus to the cross,
did it to fulfill God's great plan.
When all seemed dark and bleak to those watching
from the sidelines, the story was being woven together.
Different pieces were being fitted perfectly together
to accomplish God's perfect plan.

This season celebrate the risen Messiah, Jesus Christ,
and the promises of God that have been, are, and
will be fulfilled!

"Faith in God's promises is the only way to find
peace in the midst of trouble." -Warren Wiersbe

Thank You's and all that sappy stuff...

Special thanks to my family, who put up with hot dogs, a messy kitchen, undone laundry, and gross bathrooms during my push to finish this study the first year. And same to them again in 2016 as I drew, formatted, edited and revised for 2016.

I owe a huge thanks to my editor, Kristen, who listened to me doubt, cry, whine, and want to throw this away and give up MULTIPLE TIMES when the writing got tough. She kept encouraging and inspiring to the end with perfectly timed quotes, scripture references, or laughter. Really, the only reason this study is here now is because of her encouragement to persevere and the grace of God!

And mostly, thank you to my Savior, the Messiah from before the foundation of the earth, Jesus Christ. Thank you Jesus, for living and dying and being raised, all for me. You are God, You are King, You are my Master, my Everything.
All glory to You.

Resources

Pamphlet covering 100 prophecies fulfilled by Jesus.
http://www.rose-publishing.com/100-Prophecies-Fulfilled-By-Jesus-Pamphlet-P73.aspx#.VlHhaHarTcs

Jesus: the Greatest Life of All -Charles Swindoll
http://amzn.to/1lCtmUa

Jesus, Who is He? -Tim Lahaye
http://amzn.to/1lCtrY4

ESV Study Bible
http://amzn.to/1lCtymr

Blue Letter Bible
https://www.blueletterbible.org/

Links to songs referenced in this study

Hark! The Herald Angels Sing
https://www.youtube.com/watch?v=Xw38pGhPXIk

O Little Town of Bethlehem
https://www.youtube.com/watch?v=XQKwZRR4mcI

Angels from the Realms of Glory
https://www.youtube.com/watch?v=PrLoWt2tfqg

Silent Night:
https://www.youtube.com/watch?v=JBJY3AxtoHM

O Holy Night:
https://www.youtube.com/watch?v=e7xkA8xoQn0

Jesu, Joy of Man's Desiring
https://www.youtube.com/watch?v=iPeVIuRjUi4

O come, O come Emmanuel
https://www.youtube.com/watch?v=DPHh3nMMu-I

Come Thou Long Expected Jesus
https://www.youtube.com/watch?v=0dmO8UPlWoo

Cornerstone
https://www.youtube.com/watch?v=Q0jPmzV1CzQ

I Heard the Bells on Christmas Day
https://www.youtube.com/watch?v=RIsoALn2Aac

God Rest Ye Merry Gentlemen
https://www.youtube.com/watch?v=lzYPQfAfq0U

The First Noel
https://www.youtube.com/watch?v=9DxQNBGKsX0

A King Like This
https://www.youtube.com/watch?v=-OsAKBFtEr4

In the Bleak Midwinter
https://www.youtube.com/watch?v=MM-2Qz4hcwI

What Child is This?
https://www.youtube.com/watch?v=TOiHg5r_cmw

Light of the World
https://www.youtube.com/watch?v=_cLhaZIBSpo

Mary, Did you Know?
https://www.youtube.com/watch?v=C1DZA_TdBBI

What a Wonderful Savior
https://www.youtube.com/watch?v=RQzW3HH64ro

Hallelujah, Light Has Come
https://www.youtube.com/watch?v=SarPJv6rUiQ

Good Christian Men Rejoice
https://www.youtube.com/watch?v=QZ4M65gAvrk

Or go to my blog at www.stonesoupforfive.com and click on the "videos" tab to go to the youtube playlist.

What are your takeaways from this study? I'd absolutely LOVE to hear from you and what you've learned! Just drop me a note through email kariandcompany@comcast.net and let's talk! I read every email and try to respond to each one (though it might take a while).

You can also contact me on Facebook at:
https://www.facebook.com/StoneSoupForFive/

or follow me on instagram at:
https://www.instagram.com/kari_denker/

If you liked this study, find many more on my blog:
http://www.stonesoupforfive.com/p/store.html

One thing that has encouraged people new to journaling more than anything else is to see
pictures of other people's pages. If you would like to share your pages to encourage and
inspire others, we have a private facebook group set up at
https://www.facebook.com/groups/830142187067817/ .

If you share on social media, I'd love it if you used the hashtag **#journalanddoodle**

Find other great Bible studies like this on my website:
http://www.stonesoupforfive.com/p/store.html

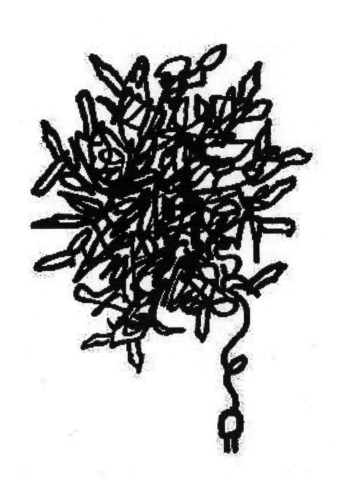

Made in the USA
Coppell, TX
27 November 2023

24846487R00061